Kirk and the Shrink Ray

Space Base gave Kirk a Shrink Ray.
The Shrink Ray made things tiny.

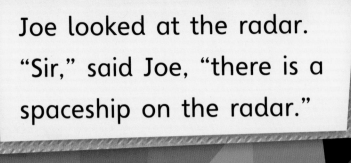

Joe looked at the radar.
"Sir," said Joe, "there is a
spaceship on the radar."

Kirk looked at the radar.
"It is Zorgon," he said. "He is
coming to steal the Shrink Ray."

"Sir," said Joe, "I have a plan. I will use the Shrink Ray to make Zorgon tiny."

Joe turned on the Shrink Ray
but he hit the wrong button.

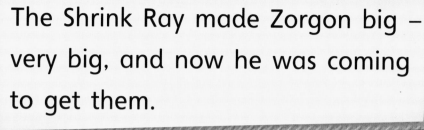

The Shrink Ray made Zorgon big –
very big, and now he was coming
to get them.

"You have hit the wrong button," said Kirk.

"Sorry, sir," said Joe.

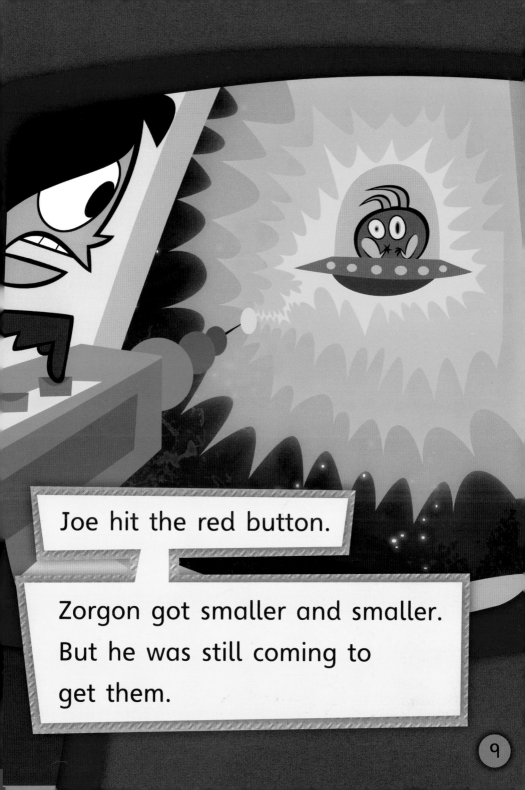

Joe hit the red button.

Zorgon got smaller and smaller.
But he was still coming to
get them.

Joe hit the red button again and again.

Zorgon got smaller and smaller. He was too small to get them.

"Just you wait," said Zorgon. "I will be back!"

"Yippee!" said Joe. "I have got rid of Zorgon!"

"Yes," said Kirk, "but now the Shrink Ray is tiny too!"

Quiz

Text Detective

- What happened when Joe first turned on the Shrink Ray?
- What do you think Kirk will do with the tiny Shrink Ray?

Word Detective

- **Phonic Focus:** Initial consonant clusters

  Page 9: Sound out the four phonemes in 'still'.
  Can you blend the first two sounds?
- Page 10: Find a word meaning the opposite of 'bigger'.
- Page 11: What word does Joe say that shows he is very happy?

Super Speller

Read these words:

tiny plan red

Now try to spell them!

HA! HA! HA!

Q What's an astronaut's favourite game?

A Astro-noughts and crosses.

Before Reading

Find out about

- Some of the biggest things in the world

Tricky words

- world
- biggest
- Robert Wadlow
- broken
- Xi Shu (say *Zee Shoo*)
- tower
- stadium
- Mount Everest
- mountain

Introduce these tricky words and help the reader when they come across them later!

Text starter

Do you know what some of the biggest things in the world are? Do you know who had the biggest hands and feet, or who the biggest man is? They hold the record today, but one day those records will be broken.

What a Whopper!

Some things in the world are big.
Some things are very big . . . and
some things are the biggest in
the world.

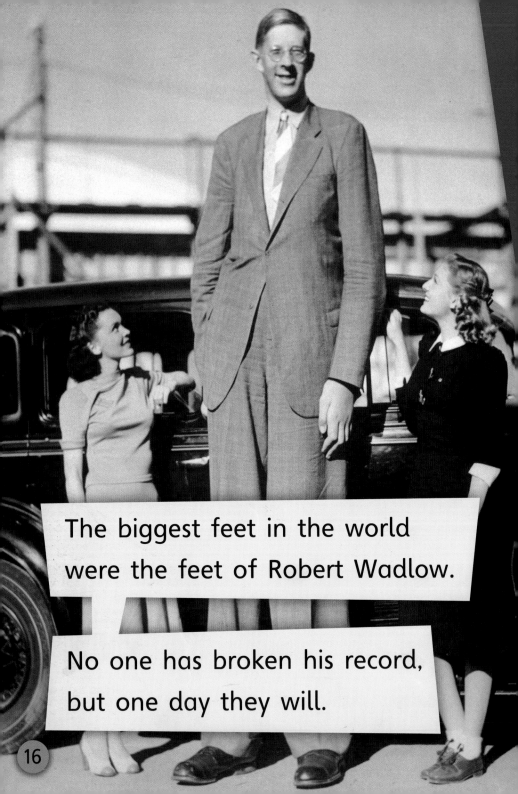

The biggest feet in the world
were the feet of Robert Wadlow.

No one has broken his record,
but one day they will.

The biggest man in the world is Xi Shu. He is 2.36 metres tall.

No one has broken his record, but one day they will.

The biggest TV in the world is 2.6 metres wide.

That is as wide as a bus!

No one has made a bigger TV, but one day they will.

The biggest tower in the world is in Canada.
It is 553 metres high.

The tower is so tall that the top sways in the wind.

No one has made a bigger tower, but one day they will.

The biggest cave in the world is in Malaysia.

It is bigger than a football stadium.

No one has found a bigger cave, but one day they will.

The biggest mountain in the world is Mount Everest.

It is over 8000 metres high.

No one has ever found a bigger mountain . . . and they never will!

Quiz

Text Detective

- Why will the Mount Everest record never be broken?
- What record would you like to hold?

Word Detective

- **Phonic Focus:** Initial consonant clusters

  Page 16: Sound out the six phonemes in 'broken'. Can you blend the first two sounds?
- Page 20: Find a word meaning 'largest'.
- Page 23: Why are there three dots after the word 'mountain'?

Super Speller

Read these words:

high bigger never

Now try to spell them!

HA! HA! HA!

Q Who can jump higher than a skyscraper?

A Anybody – skyscrapers can't jump!

24